MARK HANNA
HIS BOOK

First Edition

With an Introduction by

JOE MITCHELL CHAPPLE

BOSTON

The Chapple Publishing Co., Ltd.

1904

The Fort Hill Press

SAMUEL USHER

176 TO 184 HIGH STREET

BOSTON, MASS.

CONTENTS

INTRODUCTION

A SHORT time prior to his death, I sat at the feet of one whom I consider the greatest giver of power I have ever known among men. It was during the early hours of Sunday, in his room at the Arlington Hotel in Washington, that I sat for three hours and heard a sermon the like of which I never listened to before. There was no text from Holy Writ, but rather from the human heart was the lesson drawn. It seemed as though in those serene moments, in the quietude that always clings to the day of rest, he spoke words that were almost super-natural. His great heart seemed to well up in sympathy for humanity, as he outlined the great culminating idea of his life-work. In that hour he gave forth a message to the world that, reduced to writing and published in the *National Magazine* for February, 1904, won the appro-bation of the whole country. Those brown and brilliant eyes glistened afresh with the deep feeling that filled his breast. His words,

listened to with rapt attention, were freighted
with wisdom, affection and kindliness, impress-
ive of his greatness as a man and a statesman.
His serenity and gentleness emphasized the
grandeur of his character as husband, father,
brother, friend, statesman, philanthropist and
patriot.

As he sat there straight before his desk talking, I looked at the kind features which I had
grown to love as dearly as those of my own
father, and was struck anew with his remarkable resemblance to William McKinley ; and
somehow the thought flashed over me as I
listened in almost breathless wonder, — " Is
this to be the last message of our beloved chief-
tain? Is all this to sum up in one utterance
his final counsel and admonition to his country-
men, as did that memorable last speech of
William McKinley at Buffalo? "

I shuddered at the thought, but yet there
was in the Senator's face a pallor, and in his
frame a perceptible languor, that told how
freely and unselfishly he had given his vital
force as an offering to his country and his
fellowmen.

It was in this last talk that he told me many details of his early life — how at college he " was a boy, and a real boy at that," he playfully said. He told how he had joined in a plot to break up the junior exhibition when one of the president's sons was in the class. A copy of the program was secured, and late that night he drove into Cleveland, roused a printer out of bed and had printed a satire on " The Ubiquitous Juniors." Returning at early dawn, the problem was how to distribute the programs. After canvassing the matter in secret caucus, it was finally decided that " Mark " would have to do it. So he marched boldly into the chapel that morning with arms full of satirical matter, which he scattered like the leaves of Autumn, up one aisle and down the other, with the distinguished faculty chasing him even to his room. He was brought before the august fathers of the college, and in manly fashion told them he was the ringleader and was willing to take the consequences; but he protected his chums, who were in the meantime carrying on the well-defined plan outlined on the programs, which delightfully mixed everything up. The junior exhibition was as inglorious as even their hearts could wish, but the future Senator left college.

Later, clad in overalls and rolling pork barrels about for shipment, he was met by the president of that college. There was a cordial greeting, and young Hanna tried to impress upon his former instructor just how much the college had missed when it dispensed with his presence; but the president eyed him gravely from head to foot and said, " Well, Mark, you have just about reached your right place this time."

But those pork barrels were rolled and managed with the aggressive power and activity that characterized the statesman of a later day.

———

It was on this last Sunday that the Senator related to me one of the most touching and tender incidents of his earlier years. He prefaced it by stating that he was past twenty-five years of age before he ever tasted intoxicating liquor of any kind. During those early days when he was associated in Cleveland with high-spirited young men of ample means, his father's heart was apprehensive, as the

heart of almost every father is apt to be for
sons of tender age. The elder Hanna was rigid
and uncompromising in his total abstinence
principles, and often said he would rather see
his boy brought home in a coffin than stagger-
ing home drunk. For this reason Marcus
never had a latchkey, but every time he came
home late his father would get up and let him
in. And surely no father ever watched over a
son with more solicitude; but young Hanna
rebelled and even appealed to his mother
for a latchkey.

"Mother," said he, "you can trust me.
Whenever I touch a drop of liquor I will give
you back this key."

What a splendid proof of the confidence
between mother and son is here; and he
obtained not only the key to her home at that
time, but retained the key to her heart to her
dying day. Needless to say, he was true to
his word, and no incident in his whole life, it
seems to me, reveals the sterling worth in
the character of the man better than this.

When he related this story to Mr. Dover
and myself he especially requested that it

should never be made public during his life-
time. "Because," as he said, "these things
are apt to be misunderstood, and I prefer to
have the people appreciate me for my public
work and nothing else."

A contemporary of John D. Rockefeller, he
reached manhood in the dawn of the great
business era of the country, and the keen brown
eyes of Mark Hanna pierced the veil of the
future; his associates of those earlier days
always felt that he had a power that was
bound to win success sooner or later. As the
country evolved from the pioneer to the
developed stage, he became a business man
whose word was as good as his bond and
whose dealings were always marked by exact
justice and fairness. All these years of experience accumulated and accentuated the keen
common sense and business capacity that he
gave to the country in later years.

A young lieutenant in the Union army, he
went to the front at Bull Run, and never wavered in his patriotic devotion to his country.
At Washington he saw for the first time a

President, — the tall, gaunt figure wearing a beaver hat and shawl wound about thin shoulders. Little did he think that he would some day name a friend as Lincoln's successor.

When the megaphone rang out in the solitary woods of the Adirondacks, it called Theodore Roosevelt to be President of the United States and pledged to him the friendship of McKinley's right-hand man. When, later, in the parlor at Buffalo the oath of office was administered to Roosevelt, one of the first to pledge him unswerving loyalty and friendship in carrying out the policy of McKinley was Mark Hanna; and in all the intrigue of political warfare, in all the temptations of power and position, — with the presidency itself within his grasp, — I know, what every friend of Mark Hanna knows, that he stood firm and steadfast by his word.

It would be difficult in searching the history of nations to find a man more simple in his greatness and more honest and just in his dealings — a man so straightforward that he almost lacked tact. Prevarication of any sort was abhorrent to him; his great rugged honesty stands as an ideal for young American citizens. Like Oliver Cromwell, he came late in life into the political arena, but, unlike that stern statesman, he retained his popularity to the last moment. Senator Hanna passed away only after he had given his supreme effort to his country for peace and good will between labor and capital. He died in the harness, as he often wished to do, and departed with the well-earned laurels unwithered on his brow. If there was any one thing that he especially appreciated in his last days above all else, it was the fact that the American people had come at last to understand him. Cartooned, maligned and abused as few public men have ever been, he forgot and forgave it all in the sweet, inspiring moment of his conquest over prejudice and blind passion.

The great victory of 1903 in Ohio was a personal tribute to Mark Hanna as a man and a statesman. His popularity steadily increased since those days, as was shown by the many messages of love and admiration that were sent to him during the last few months of his life from all parts of the country. And they were a great source of gratification, not to his vanity, — for he had none of that, — but rather to his patriotism and his great human heart; for it was sweet to know that the country that he loved reciprocated that affection. From the North and from all portions of the South, from the Lone Star State especially, from the great West and the calmer but not colder East, came showers of tributes of love and admiration, such words as have seldom been as freely bestowed upon any statesman; and yet through it all he remained the same, — simple, sweet, candid, but of positive opinions and honest always.

———

I must here and now pay my personal tribute by saying that the success of the *National Magazine* was made possible through Senator Hanna. It was he who gave the first friendly grasp of the hand and insisted that it could be made a success. It was he who withstood all other offers of larger and greater publications to become a contributor, preferring rather to give what he intended to write to those whom he felt it would most help. And from the

moment that his first article on " McKinley as
I Knew Him " was published in the *National
Magazine*, the growth and prosperity of that
periodical seemed assured. His only protest
to me was, " Don't put so much ' Hanna ' in
the *National!* " And when I insisted that
that was what made the magazine popular,
he would blush like a boy and declare that if
I persisted he would sever all relations with
me.

Among the treasures that I possess are the
first pages of the article on '' McKinley as I
Knew Him,'' written by Mark Hanna for the
National Magazine, and which was, in fact,
the first contribution he ever made to any
periodical. There is something pathetic in
these first pages, indicating the difficulty he
had in writing about his friend in such a manner as to do him such justice as may be done
by human judgment. These pages had been
torn up and cast aside in the waste-basket as
worthless when I rescued them; but they serve,
to my mind, to show the courage and persist-
ence of the man in accomplishing what he had
undertaken, and not only the accomplishment

but in not being satisfied with less than his " level best." That all this work was done as a labor of love there can be no doubt; and this and all his writings show that, though he entered this field late in life, he had sterling natural gifts as a writer. The simplicity and lucidity of his style make his writings more valuable than many more ornate compositions; and in all he wrote there was the simplicity and sincerity that wins the hearts of the great American people for whom he wrote.

———

I can never forget the day following the death of William McKinley, when, with tears streaming down his face, the Senator told me of the keen sense of loss and loneliness that lay like a pall upon him; nor how, in all he ever said or wrote of his friend, he never took the slightest credit to himself for any part of McKinley's greatness. His own efforts were but as the dust in the balance, compared with his friend's excellence. Many a time as we traveled together, as the train flew on its way, the time to me flew even faster listening to such " tales sublime " as might well grace the pages of the greatest history.

I recall also what an inspiration there was in his cheering face in the moment of despair or difficulty, and how that face lit up when the hour of victory came for his friends. I well remember his radiant face at the Philadelphia Convention, in 1900, when, as chairman, he waved the great plumes incessantly for ten or fifteen minutes while the throng of people cheered for William McKinley. And as I climbed on the platform during a moment of chaos, he turned to me and, with his eyes glistening, cried: " You here, Joe? Isn't this glorious? Take a plume and whoop 'er up!"

After the convention adjourned we held converse in husky voices, and he brought forth a box of trophies with the remark, " Now we want to get right out for the campaign."

It was my good fortune to meet him frequently during the last years of his life; and while he was admonishing me to ease the pace at which I was going, there was he setting me a pace, in his sixty-sixth year, that it was impossible for me to keep up to, in the matter of traveling. First he was at the Civic Federation meeting in Chicago, spending hours in earnest conference with the labor leaders; within a day or two, perhaps, at a leading financial meeting in New York; the day following, taking his simple luncheon in his office in Cleveland, because he had not time for a regular midday meal; then at a directors' meeting, and half a dozen other meetings, but never for one moment losing his grasp on the chief factors in his program.

In all the years in which he was engaged in business, no word against him was ever uttered by the real workingmen. The idlers, it is true, did not admire him. Why was it that the great factories were stopped during the last illness of this man, and that thousands of men would leave their work unfinished at the desk or bench to get one word of possible comfort or hope as to his welfare, or at least to ask assurance that he was still living? Was ever tribute paid to any American more touching than this? And what more is needed to indicate where the great mission of Senator Hanna lay, or what his great lifework was? His last, best efforts were given to the closing

of the breach between labor and capital; this
work of his is not only fairly begun, but it is
well done and will last for all time as the
foundation stone on which the future edifice
may stand with safety.   His influence it was
that brought broader ideas to both sides in the
conflict, and especially does his lifework stand
for humane and just treatment of employees.
As the scroll of history unfolds and shows how
this great problem has confronted our nation
in the dawn of the twentieth century, the
fruition of the hopes that Marcus A. Hanna
carried to his dying day will be realized in the
sound adjustment of this vexed question.

It was in the office of the Auditorium at
Chicago, after he had returned from a weari-
some meeting of the Civic Federation, that
I sat down for a smoke and talk in an obscure
corner with Mr. Hanna. Presently a Salvation Army lass came along, rattling her tambourine for quarters, or pence, as the case
might be.   The Senator glanced up and saw
who she was, then placed a contribution in the

tambourine that made mine look like thirty cents. Pretty soon she came back.

"Why, sir, did you know that this was a ten-dollar bill?"

"Yes," he said; "I knew it. You belong to my church."

Then she looked a little closer.

"Why, it is Senator Hanna!" she cried, and that explained it all. Nothing more was necessary, for if the Salvation Army ever had a true friend, it had one in Senator Hanna. During the visit of General Booth to this country it was the Senator who gave the famous dinner at the Arlington, where the great leader of the Salvation Army related such touching incidents that he drew tears from the eyes of the guests. It was Mark Hanna who had this great leader offer a prayer and benediction in the Senate that sent a thrill through all who heard — a distinguished circle of senators, diplomats and statesmen.

———

The life of Senator Hanna, more than that of any other prominent man, seemed to typify the American life of to-day. He understood

intimately and sympathetically all phases of the
varied needs of the people.   It was an inspiration to have such a leader.   He was a captain
of industry in the true sense of the term.   He
was also a statesman in all that the modern
use of the word implies, showing equally broad
comprehension and versatility on political problems and business propositions.   He recognized
business as the genius of the age, and was not
blind to any of the salient points of a proposition, notwithstanding they might be offset by
sentimental side issues.   It was a picture to be
remembered to see him enter the Senate with
his little cane, and limp to his seat, serene and
strong, "four square to every wind that blew."
To see his confrères gathered about him after a
great victory — such as when, with a single brief
speech, he reversed the vote of the Senate on the
Isthmian Canal question, conquering through
the sheer force of his honesty and integrity,
acknowledged alike by partisans and opponents
— was an inspiration indeed.

———

I liked to see him on a hot summer day in
his office at Cleveland, far above the seething,

smoking heat of the factory, working away in his shirt sleeves with all the vigor and energy of a man in his prime. I have often noticed that he never sat sidewise at his desk, but tackled his work square front, and erect.

A visit to his beautiful Cleveland home, "Lake View," was a rare treat indeed. It was as a host that Mark Hanna was at his very best; it was to this home that President McKinley loved to come during the trying days that preceded his election to the presidency. That home is the Mecca of all Hanna's admirers — rich, yet simple and tasteful, in harmony with the spirit of its master. It was in the library here that he gave me the soundest advice I have ever received. He loved mankind, and his every act bore witness to that sentiment. I think that in the walks I had with him I came to know him best, for he was capable of inspiring and satisfying friendship in the highest meaning of the word; and during these quiet hours I heard from his lips words freighted with deep thoughts, full of the tender solicitude that a father might show a son or a man younger than himself who had yet to live

through the struggle that he had passed over
so successfully.   In the briefest phrases, sometimes, in disconnected sentences, the innate
feelings of the man were revealed, interspersed
with flashes of wit and humor.

———

I have not spoken of his keen insight into
character and his remarkable faculty for choos-
ing the right men to help in his great undertak-
ings.   Notable among those so selected is his
private secretary, Elmer Dover, now secretary
of the Republican National Committee, than
whom a more loyal, faithful and capable secretary never lived. As the Senator's political
work increased, to say nothing of his business
enterprises, the tremendous load must have
swamped him but for the constant, careful attention of Mr. Dover, whose perfect knowledge
of all Mr. Hanna's affairs made it difficult to
distinguish the work of the one from the other.
In view of the hundreds of letters and tele-
grams that came daily to him, it was often
necessary for Mr. Dover to use the signature
of his chief: and in one instance where this was
done a lady wrote back saying that she could

read the character of the Senator from his signature; but Mr. Hanna laughingly insisted that this noble character must belong, not to himself, but to Mr. Dover, who had signed the letter. There can be no doubt as to Mr. Hanna's appreciation of his secretary. There seemed to be a most perfect understanding between the two men.

———

Those who were with him in the campaign of 1896 will never forget the tireless vigor, the alertness, the swift decision of the great political captain. A conference with Senator Hanna always meant business. He had the art of bringing all the vital points into focus in a short time. He seemed to sweep the whole battle-field at a glance, and never appeared to overlook the smallest detail. The same man who went among his employees with " Hello, Pete," " Hello, Jack. How's the family? " and with his joke and laugh brought out the best that was in them, inspired the same personal and unflinching loyalty in his lieutenants. No hour too late, no day too hot, no time too valuable to find the Senator prepared for the duty before him. He often quoted to me the words of St. Paul: " This one thing I *do*," which seemed to have especially directed him, for he was preeminently a *doer*.

———

While occupying the historic Cameron House on Lafayette Square in Washington, the former home of Secretary Seward, there was a " continuous performance," to quote from the vaudeville, in the early days of the McKinley administration, that was decidedly picturesque. The Senator would come down from breakfast to find an assemblage awaiting him. Puffing his black cigar and switching the little cane he always carried, he recognized every man in the anteroom and had a cordial word for each friend seated around on the old-fashioned chairs with their covering of flowered brocade. The same impartiality was in his manner whether he spoke to the man of millions or the workingman.

At eleven o'clock he was always promptly in the committee-room, usually reaching the Capitol by means of the street cars. He seemed never to lose a minute, but spent all his time in holding conferences or grappling single-handed with some problem. On returning from the Senate in the afternoon he would square around to his desk, and with his own hand write such letters as he felt could not be dictated. Among my treasures I cherish several of these letters as priceless possessions. He continued to work until dusk; interruptions never seemed to trouble him, as he could at once pick up the thread of his thoughts again.

It is a curious fact that in all these years of public life he never kept a scrapbook, and no public man could be more indifferent than he was to adulation in print. Once he was reading an anecdote which had been published about him, in which he was represented as quoting from the classics.

" Now, what do you think of that?" he turned to me and asked. " Classics! I never knew anything about classics, and that fellow must have a mighty good imagination." A few minutes later his old teacher came in, Professor White, a venerable gentleman of about four-score years. There was a hearty hand grasp, and the old gentleman said:

" The same irrepressible Mark! Why, Mark, you were the most classical scholar I had in the old schoolhouse, and I always felt you had a classical genius for *doing* things." They talked over old days until I could almost see the old place and the girls and boys, and the refrain of time-honored songs rang in my ears.

―――――

Once during the campaign of 1896, when McKinley was speaking day after day to the throngs who made pilgrimages to Canton — and days had passed since he had seen the captain of his forces — he decided to call him up on the telephone. His first inquiry was:

" Is that you, Mark? "

" Yes, Mr. President-to-be," was the answer in a confident voice.

" Well, Mark, am I doing all right?" came the query.

" Doing all right! " came the exclamation. " Why, Major, you have set the pace that will lead us to the greatest victory the party has ever had. Doing all right? Why, I find that I will not have to write any more of your speeches that the newspapers give me credit for."

" How do you like your pictures in the papers? " asked McKinley.

" I haven't looked for my picture," was the answer; " it is your picture that we want the people to see."

Almost every one who talked with the Senator for a half hour remembers some flash of humor, some joke. How well I recall finding him in his office last summer wearing a handsome bouquet in his buttonhole. He saw us glancing at it, and smilingly remarked that these were the laurels he had won the night before, and went on to relate how he had just made an address to college girls and had told them that he always preferred women for office work. " And I meant it, too," he added.

———

There was a pathetic interest in one of the latest callers the Senator received at the Arlington, — an old German who came to bring the greetings and love of his German community; and the good man in his broken speech insisted that the Senator would some day dwell in the White House.

" Why, Peter," answered Mr. Hanna, " that

would kill me. I could never stand the campaign, much less the duties of the office."

" Vell," said Peter, " Zenator, you might die in the White House."

" Well, Peter," replied the Senator, " I have no wish to die either at the White House or elsewhere just yet. I have too much to do, and I would rather live to see the problem settled between labor and capital than be President or anything else."

" Vell," was the answer, " if you won't be President, we vant you to lif long as our Zenator. We luf you in our hearts."

———

Death has called another friend, but somehow, even in the depth and keenness of first grief, in the sense of loss of that warm hand grasp, in the obliterated light of those bright eyes, we see some hope gleaming and take courage to place upon the bier a chaplet of immortelles that will symbolize the undying memory of the great man, the wise statesman, the devoted husband, father and brother, the true friend, the brilliant financier, the noble philanthropist, the business man of unimpeachable integrity, and, finally, that greatest tribute that can be paid to an American, the great Citizen, truly a citizen in the perfect meaning of the word, Marcus Alonzo Hanna.

JOE MITCHELL CHAPPLE.

SOCIALISM AND THE LABOR UNIONS

I HAVE always been a firm believer in the power of education, whether in politics, religion or business, and there has never been a people more susceptible to the power and influence of education than the American people. Although I came upon the political field rather late in life, I was deeply impressed by the wonderful manner in which the people of this country can be made to understand a direct, logical proposition. The campaign of 1896 was to me an education, and brought home the belief that human nature is pretty much the same all the world over; that the fundamental basis of right success, as it appears to me, is fairness and justice; and that the simpler the proposition can be made, the more effective it is going to be with the people at large.

There is no more engrossing question than that of the relation between labor and capital, which seems the paramount issue to-day. In the dawn of a new century, looking back over our history, we are almost bewildered by the great and wonderful progress of the country; and no matter how we may demur against the changes that are thrusting themselves upon us, we must, sooner or later, grapple with the question — the serious problem — of the adjustment of these matters, instead of trying to turn back to conditions that have passed. Is it not better courageously and manfully to face the proposition of the future, and make an united effort to settle it? With our beloved country possessed of greater physical advantages than any other portion of the globe, possessed of the benefits of a cosmopolitan population, standing foremost in the ranks of social industry and advancement, we have a heavy responsibility in proportion to the blessings we enjoy. The tendency has been to study economics purely from a political standpoint, and my experience has led me to believe that there are social and moral phases of the relations between labor and capital often lost sight of in the eager pursuit of gain. My attention was called to these things after the

great strike in the coal mines of Ohio, in which
I was indirectly interested, and it was then that
I concluded that the first thing to be done was
to adjust conditions in a straightforward manner.

It cannot be denied that there was a popular
prejudice against union labor as an imported
article. It came to us with the tide of im-
migration from the Old World, where it was
bred among conditions which do not and cannot exist in America, where the mighty advantages of popular education are free to all.

It must never be forgotten that organized
labor is an older institution than organized
capital. The instinct of workingmen to band
together to protect themselves is no more to
be wondered at than the same instinct when
shown on the part of capital. Now, my plan
is to have organized union labor Americanized
in the best sense and thoroughly educated to
an understanding of its responsibilities, and in
this way to make it the ally of the capitalist,
rather than a foe with which to grapple.

It is often asked what is to become of the
non-organized consumer if an amicable alliance

is made between labor and capital. But there is no such middle group as this question implies. There is no other group than that of either labor or capital — every man belongs either to the one or the other, when you stop to think of it; for that matter, he is likely to belong to both.

The systematic work of education was begun during the past five years by the Civic Federation. I took some time to consider the work of the Federation, and am firmly convinced that it is the object to which I desire to consecrate the remaining years of my life. I fully appreciate that it is a long struggle, but the progress already made under the motto of the Civic Federation — the Golden Rule — has surpassed even my most sanguine expectations; and I am sure that the American people will sustain a policy, based upon the highest moral and social impulse, which will eliminate the passionate prejudices that now exist between capital and labor.

We oppose the sympathetic strike, and this view was most heroically endorsed by the action of the Mine Workers' Association at

Indianapolis during the great coal-mine strike
in Pennsylvania ; we oppose also the boy-
cott ; we disapprove of the restriction of pro-
duction to enhance values — and all these be-
liefs are being gradually adopted, not only by
union labor, but by cool-headed and far-seeing
representatives of capital. The decayed code
of principles and policy that has no true harmony with the spirit of the age — which is
Business — is passing away.   It is so easy on
the floor of a convention for one or two inflam-
matory speakers to set on fire the passions of
their hearers, whereas the mature deliberations
of the committee will hold in check such
feelings as might otherwise be fanned into revo-
lution.   It must be considered that hereto-
fore big capitalists, or the employing interests,
have had the advantage, because there were
more workmen than there was work.   But
conditions have changed, and for every work-
man, on an average, there are two jobs now
in the heyday of our prosperity ; and it is ex-
pecting too much of human nature to suppose
that workingmen shall not desire a larger share
of the profits.   Has not this motive been the

stimulating incentive of the men who are managing business affairs? We cannot justly expect more from the man who has not been educated on the side of capital than we do from those who are thinkers and scholars, and have inherited these qualities for generations; and no one who is acquainted with union labor for the past five years can fail to recognize the wonderful advancement that has been made in conservative, cool-headed and thoroughly practical management of these matters by the workingmen themselves. This is coming to be more and more realized as the one great purpose in union labor, and when the men in that great mine-workers' convention decided to adopt the report of the committee, after it had struggled through an all-night session, and then manfully stood by their word unanimously, it cast a ray of light on a difficult problem, and also enlisted the interest and sympathy of the American people in the welfare of these toilers in the dark.

Every man is vulnerable in some part, and it is a rare thing to find any man proof against methods of kindness and justice. Labor or-

ganizations may be open to sharp criticism
at times, but it cannot be fairly stated that
they are always wrong. If every man is
treated as a *man*, and an appeal made to his
heart, as well as to his reason, it will establish
a bond of confidence as a sure foundation to
build upon. This is the condition that is
aimed at by the Civic Federation — absolute
confidence on both sides. Many of the ills
that have crept into labor organizations are
importations from older countries and will not
live here because they are not fitted to our
conditions. While labor unions may have
been a curse to England, I believe that they
will prove a boon to our own country, when
a proper basis of confidence and respect is established. We have, perhaps, been too busy
and too engrossed in our rapid expansion to
look upon the ethical side of this question, and
forgot that two factors contributed to the prosperity of our nation, — the man who works
with his hands and the man who works with
his head, — partners in toil who ought to be
partners also in the profits of that toil.

All strikes do not originate in a demand

for higher wages. There are other grievances. With the great army of employees necessary to our industrial institutions it is quite impossible for each individual to receive such close consideration at the hands of his employer as in earlier days might have been accorded, and it is to meet this condition that we have to adopt the propositions of union labor, and press forward the campaign of education, which means reason on both sides, though it is too much to expect altogether to change the great current of selfishness on both sides. If there are enough people actuated by the right motives it can be done in a great measure, and a feeling of fellowship established that will obviate to a large extent the disastrous effects of the strike.

We must make the hundreds of thousands coming from a lower social condition in the Old World feel that prejudice against the government is futile and unnecessary, and that they have a large share of the responsibility for the wise ordering of business conditions. All this takes time. Coming to us unlettered and untaught, it remains for us to show what we can do for the next generation, and it is to them we must look to properly assimilate and carry out the American ideals of trade and industry.

It is truly astonishing to consider what trivial disagreements have occasioned some of the most serious strikes. I have seen two parties stand apart, each with a chip on his shoulder, defying his opponent to knock it off, and moved by emotions and considerations that were very far from promoting the welfare of either party. There is more to overcome in the way of feeling on the part of capital than on the part of labor. Capital has been for many generations entrenched behind its power to dictate conditions, whether right or wrong, and the abrogation of this power is not going to weaken, in the least degree, the strength ot the hitherto dominant party, for no better investment exists for a manufacturing institution or a corporation than the hearty cooperation and good feeling of the employees. If we go upon this hypothesis, it seems to me quite possible that all differences may be obviated in the future by the proverbial ounce of prevention which is worth a pound of cure. As in our national legislation, and in successful business corporations, a large part of the best initiative comes from the careful deliberations of the committee-room and the conference, so may this national and almost universal question be met and successfully settled in the same way.

The menace of today, as I view it, is the spread of a spirit of socialism, one of those things which is only half understood and is more or less used to inflame the popular mind against all individual initiative and personal energy, which has been the very essence of American progress. While this spirit of socialism has caused apprehension in some quarters, it has been joyfully received by a certain class of people who do not desire to acquire competence in the ordinary and honest manner, and gladly seize any excuse for agitating the public mind, on the chance of putting money in their own pockets,—the men who are described as having " no stake in the country."

My own impression is confirmed by information from laboring men, that socialism, in the

European sense of the word, will never find a
firm footing in America. There is a spirit of
cooperation or community of interests which
some people may confound with socialism
that is making headway with us; but when
any one attempts, for political or financial
reasons, to advocate the whole program of
European socialism, he will find little prospect
of the seed taking root in American soil.
This, I think, was demonstrated very conclu-
sively in the Ohio campaign, where higher
socialism was brought forth as an issue. When
the people understand this subject in its full-
est sense and some of the mysteries and the
fascinating glamor connected with the mysterious that now shroud the subject are torn
away, and it is seen plainly, it will be found
to be repellent to American ideas of integrity
and honesty. Its objects will be seen to be
the very opposite of those desired both by
labor and capital, since it gives no aid toward
the building up and development of the
country, nor does it guarantee each man a
chance to make a home for himself. Fairness
and justice will never agree to the confiscation

Fear of Socialism
taking private things away

of the products of one man's toil in order to
insure comfort to the idle and worthless. The
old law of compensation is operative now as
ever. No " ism " is wanted by the American
people that will take from any citizen the just
and equitable reward of his labor. There is
always a likelihood of movements of this kind
fascinating people who have met with a degree
of failure in their own efforts; but it is a short-
sighted policy to destroy the fabric of national
union in order to promulgate a doctrine the
very essence of which is selfishness. I believe
a single vigorous campaign of agitation would
quickly show what support these doctrines
may expect from the American people, as has
been proven over and over along these lines.
As a general rule, the American people are
pretty level-headed.

Now, I do not mean that those who have
taken up socialism should be roundly scored
and abused, for a great many of these are
honest and sincere in their belief, which belief
arises from not really understanding the matter, having been misled by misrepresentation.
It is usually said that there are only two sides

to a question, but in this matter there are two
sides and two ends, and by the time our social-
ist has surveyed the two sides and the big end
and the little one, he will not find that socialism is going to benefit him much in America.

It seems to me more reasonable to take up
the difficulties of labor and capital case by
case, and situation after situation, as they come
up, and try to adjust them in a manner at
once permanent and peaceful; in this way the
inherent rights of the individual will be better
served than by an attempt to demolish a system of government which is so well suited to
the needs of the American people and which
has so well withstood the attacks of the dreamer
and the agitator in the years that are past.

If there is any one superb virtue that the
American people possess it is courage in grappling with the issues of the future, and I do
not think there will ever be a faltering note
in this respect, no matter what the obstacle,
no matter what the difficulty may be. But
we must get right down to the belief that life
is a matter of mutual interest between labor
and capital; we cannot separate the two great

factors which underlie our development; it is not possible for one to prosper permanently unless the other shares in that prosperity. There must be a common ground where all can meet with the honest determination to do what is right, meeting bravely the conditions as they change and seizing the opportunity as it offers for the betterment of all the people. The movement already inaugurated among large employers looking toward the utmost comfort and convenience of their employees is not carried out altogether from philanthropic motives but is a matter of business also, and it is one of the most hopeful signs of the times.

This is essentially a great economic age — an age when energy, materials and purposes are all being utilized for the best. When a man loses his day's work, and is compelled to spend that time in absolute idleness, the whole community suffers a loss as well as he, and it is something that is lost forever to the commonwealth; this would be found entirely unnecessary were the honest motives of both sides given proper consideration. And we feel convinced that we have a very great duty

to perform in resisting the onslaught of the
socialistic tendency which helps to bring this
state of affairs into being.   Both capital and
labor must yield in time to the great law of
fair dealing, man to man.   In proportion to
a man's ambitions and his ability to earn for
himself a betterment of his condition, there
will be a striving on his part to attain his ideals,
and this, in itself, is the germ of progress; and
just as far as that encroaches on others who
are working for the same object there will be
a natural resistance.   But there are few citizens in this country who would condone any
interference with the personal rights of a neigh-
bor.   There always will be a neutral ground
where conflicting interests can meet and con-
fer and adjust themselves — a sort of Hague
tribunal, if you please, in the everyday affairs
of life.

The American labor unions are becoming
more and more conservative and careful in
their management, and are not likely to be
led away from the straight road by hot-headed
members.

Business men, too, have found that fighting

does not pay in trade. There is an old saying that the best lawyer is he who keeps his client out of lawsuits, and the best leader is he who can avoid difficulties; but the greater experience and intelligence which necessarily exist among employers, owing to the fact of their longer training in the forum of business, places upon them an important responsibility.

I wish I could impress upon every American the individual responsibility that rests upon each one of us. Every year of experience, every dollar of accumulated capital, every talent we possess should be regarded as a sacred charge for the good of the nation, to help in uniting the interests of rich and poor, learned and unlearned.

WILLIAM McKINLEY AS I KNEW HIM

I. His Masterly Campaigns

It is something over thirty years ago that I first knew William McKinley, a young practicing attorney at Canton, Ohio. Strange as it may seem, I cannot recall the exact time or place when I first met him. I know that it was early in the seventies, and I have a recollection of being strangely attracted to the quiet and methodical lawyer. Our acquaintance was somewhat closer after his election to Congress and in some way I always felt a personal interest in his contests from time to time. Our acquaintanceship was a simple growth of friendship. His splendid work in the cause of Protection as a congressman further attracted me. This was even before he had reached prominence in Congress as a member of the Ways and Means Committee. I never thought of the possibility at that time of his becoming a candidate for the presidency, and

Hunn

was not especially active in politics except in so far as exercising my influence in the interests of the Republican party. Our first association politically was in 1880, when Ohio took a prominent part in the campaign in which Garfield was elected. In 1884 William McKinley was elected delegate at large to the Republican National Convention, and I was also a delegate. McKinley was an enthusiastic supporter of Blaine, and I was for John Sherman, and we contested the delegation vigorously for our men. In the national convention of 1888 we were present again as delegates, but this time we were both pledged for John Sherman, and it was at this time McKinley made the famous speech which I felt destined him as a marked man for President.

Even before this our friendship had seemed to grow into something more than that of ordinary personal or political associates. Somehow I felt for him an affection that cannot be explained, and it was at this convention that I gained an insight into the unselfish, unfaltering loyalty which William McKinley gave to every cause he espoused.

During that convention we occupied the same rooms, and were in conference day and night as to the best ways and means to bring about the nomination of John Sherman, Ohio's Grand Old Man.

I sat by McKinley's side when he eloquently demanded that his name be withdrawn for his own honor's sake, and history records that he did withdraw it.

It was in the convention of 1888 that William McKinley developed into a positive national force. Blaine and Sherman had been in their full vigor in 1884, and I had the clear impression from that time that every turn of the wheel brought McKinley into a fuller measure of merited prominence. It was after a very hot day during the Chicago convention that General Ben Butterworth, Major McKinley and myself sat at a table talking over the events of the day. The delegates had brought forward his name. McKinley took a telegraph blank from the table, and during the moments of silence wrote down some memorable words. He passed it to me with the remark, " If this thing is repeated tomorrow, that is what I am going to say":

"I am here as one of the chosen representatives from my state. I am here by resolution of the Republican convention, cast without one dissenting vote, commanding me to vote for John Sherman and use every worthy endeavor for his nomination. I accepted the trust because my heart and judgment were in accord with the letter, spirit and purpose of that resolution. It has pleased certain delegates to cast their vote for me. I am not insensible to the honor they would do me, but in the presence of the duty resting upon me I cannot remain silent with honor. I cannot consistently with the credit of the state whose credentials I bear and which has trusted me, — I cannot with honorable fidelity to John Sherman, who has trusted me in his cause and with his confidence, — I cannot consistently with my own views of my personal integrity, consent or seem to consent to permit my name to be used as a candidate before this convention. I would not respect myself if I could find it in my heart to do, to say or to permit to be done that which could ever be ground for any one to suspect that I wavered in my loyalty to Ohio, or my devotion to the chief of her choice and the chief of mine. I do request, I demand, that no delegate who would not cast reflections on me should cast a ballot for me."

His name was brought forward the following day. Pleading loyal allegiance to John Sherman, he uttered with all the deep sincerity of the man a declaration that will live in all political history. It revealed the true loyalty and unselfishness of the man, and won for him friends and supporters who afterward joined their hands in making him President.

He was always, from his earliest political career, such a willing worker that when I remonstrated with him he would laughingly remark, " A good soldier must always be ready for duty."

His utterances in that convention are the best index to his character that I know of, and displayed in him those rare qualities of manhood which convinced me that he was destined to become a great power in national politics. And here, for the first time, it occurred to me that he was a logical candidate for the presidency in years to come. I was with him in 1892 at Minneapolis, and, as it will be remembered, the demand from the people for McKinley as a candidate was even more outspoken and seemingly irresistible than at the

previous convention. The situation was such
that it would have been an easy matter for
him to have spoken and won the entire support of the Blaine men, to say nothing of his
many admirers among those pledged for Har-
rison. At this time it was evident to even the
most casual observer that sooner or later he
would be placed in that high position for which
his talent and particular abilities qualified him.

The demonstration at Minneapolis convinced me that, although it was an impolitic
thing for his interests to nominate him there,
in the next national convention the popular
demand for his candidacy would override all
opposition.

———

The condition of the country that followed
the election of 1892 so clearly defined him as
the one man of all others in public life to lead
the Republican party that I felt that his nomination was assured.

As early as 1894 I began to feel the pulse of
the people, that is, the rank and file, business men, laboring men, traveling men and
manufacturers, to learn how far the sentiment

for McKinley had taken hold. It required only the opportunity for the people of the Northern states to express their sentiment on the subject, and the result at St. Louis justified the expectations of his friends and admirers, and gave proof of the correctness of their judgment in believing him to be the one man who fitted the situation and insured the the success of the party.

In the management of the campaign which followed I was made to appreciate how much McKinley's strong and noble personality contributed to its success. How eminently serviceable was the part which he took in meeting on his porch at Canton the people who came in throngs and thousands to greet him, no one can estimate. He not only impressed them by the earnestness and sincerity of his speeches and the wisdom of his words, but there was always present the genial personality of the man that quickly won admiration and respect from everyone with whom he came into contact. No committee organization could have furnished this great attribute of personal strength which was so necessary to the success of the ticket, and none other than such a personality could have inspired individuals in all parts of the country to do their utmost in every way to secure his election. His entire and complete confidence in those who were conducting the affairs of the campaign stimulated them to their utmost efforts, inspiring in them a desire to show their appreciation of this confidence and trust in them. I don't believe that any other political campaign in the history of the Republican party ever demonstrated such a growing interest and enthusiasm, and above all, confidence, in the personality of the candidate, which continued to grow and increase from the opening of the campaign to the great climax of Flag Day, which marked an epoch in the campaign of 1896.

It must also be remembered that his supporters were not confined to those who had hitherto always been identified with the Republican party. The others who joined us in the contest for the principles on which McKinley stood were equally enthusiastic in their admiration of the man.

The country knows today how well he filled the expectations of all those who supported him. In the earlier days of 1896, confronted as we were by unexpected developments in the silver question, — four years of depression and an industrial paralysis which resulted disastrously to all classes, when those who were suffering were looking for relief, and the proposition was made for free and unlimited coinage of silver, on the plea that the expansion of the circulating medium would make better times — under such conditions it is not strange that we found in the Republican ranks an uncertainty as to what course to pursue. It became evident that the work before us was a campaign of education of great magnitude, the results of which must necessarily be slow to accomplish.

If there were any dark days in the campaign, it was during the earlier weeks of the work. It was at that time that William McKinley in his conversation with us showed his buoyant spirit and his strong faith in the common people of the country, believing that they would meet and solve the question right and endorse the principles which were to bring relief to all. He insisted that all that was necessary was to make them understand the cause and effect of the principles advocated by both parties.

It was during the middle stage of the campaign that the results coming in indicated that the people were reading, thinking and determining conclusions for themselves. They were beginning to see where their interests were at stake. All this was the confirmation of William McKinley's faith in the people, and it was the joy of his heart to feel that he could read aright the signs of the times and that the end would justify his faith in the final judgment of the people.

His victory was greater in its proof of the faith of the people in him than merely in the choice of him as President of the United States. This was the subject that in after years we often talked about, and it was a beautiful thing to me to see how much he realized and appreciated the confidence which had come to him as a result of his abiding faith in the people. If there had been no other motive, this was the great incentive for him to use all the power and talent with which he had been endowed to give the people in return for their confidence his best life-work. And he consecrated the best efforts of his life to fulfill their expectations.

My associations with him during the years of executive life gave me further opportunity to appreciate as I never had before the great reserve force which he possessed. He seems to have met every emergency and the unusual problems and annoying complications of the times in a masterful way. These conditions furnished the opportunity for him to demonstrate his enormous talent and ability successfully to solve every problem, rising to the full measure of every situation and overcoming all obstacles.

And then the summing of it all in that beautiful death, which was so characteristic of his career, is one almost unequaled in history. He had won the admiration, love and respect of all classes of his own people, and of all nations.

There was one phrase used when we first

opened the campaign for him that seemed
to fit the situation, and that was the claim
that he was the " logical candidate." In
the first place, he marked out for himself a
distinctive political career. He had spent
every energy and used every effort in all his
public service for the highest and best interests of his people, inspired always by patriotic
impulse, with a sincerity never questioned.
His election to an office always meant more
than the mere gratification of a selfish political
ambition. He said to me once — and I cite
it here to show that his ambitions never sprang
from selfish motives — in speaking about some
of the methods adopted in contests for the
nomination, " There are some things, Mark,
I would not do and cannot do, even to become
President of the United States," and it was
my impression at that time that he himself
had little thought or idea that he would ever
be nominated for President.

A great deal has been said about his proverbial good nature. He had that, and in
addition to that an unequaled equipoise in

every emergency. In all my career, in business and in politics, I have never known a man so self-contained. He always acted deliberately, and his judgments were always weighed carefully, although there were times when his heart impulses would respond quickly, without apparently the slightest delay. In all those thirty years of close relations, I never saw him in a passion, never heard him utter one word of what I would call resentment, tinged with bitterness, toward a living person. This was again reflected in the story of the assassination told by Mr. Milburn, who said that he could never forget the picture in the expression of his countenance as he glanced toward the dastard assassin. In his eyes were the words as plain as language could express it, " Why should you do this? " And then when the assassin was hurled to the ground, when the fury and indignation of the people had begun to assert itself, he said with almost saintly compassion, " Don't let them hurt him."

I know of nothing in all history that can compare with the splendid climax and ending

of this noble life. One of the sweetest conso-
lations that come to me is the memory that on
Tuesday, preceding his death, he asked to see
a newspaper, and when he was told, " Not
today," he asked, " Is Mark here? "

" Yes, Mr. President," was the response,
and in that one sweet last remembrance was a
rich reward for the years of devotion which it
had always been my pleasure to give him.

———

It is difficult for me to express the extent
of the love and respect which I, in common
with many others, felt for him personally. The
feeling was the outgrowth of an appreciation
of his noble, self-sacrificing nature. My affection for him and faith and confidence in him
always seemed to be reciprocated, to the extent that there was never an unpleasant word
passed between us, and the history of his administration, his cabinet and his associations
with public men, so entirely free from intrigue
or base selfishness, I think will be a splendid
example to the youth of the coming generations. There was nothing in the expression of
his face or manner denoting exultation over

his victory when it was announced that he was
elected President.   He seemed to realize fully
the sacred responsibilities placed upon him,
and the quiet dignity and self-possession which
marked the man then and in days after were
just what his personal friends expected of him.
The first day I greeted him after he was inaugurated at the White House, in the course
of our conversation, I inadvertently called
him " Major " and " Governor," and when I
stopped to correct myself, he would say, " Each
one is fitting; I'm not particular which."

We were both of Scotch-Irish descent, but
opposites in disposition.   He was of a more
direct descent than I, but it is thought from
our dispositions that he had the Scotch and I
had the Irish of the combination.

II. GLIMPSES OF HIS PERSONALITY

The one absorbing purpose in William
McKinley's political career was to keep
closely in touch with the people, so that
he might promote their material and moral
welfare.

He seemed to study and watch current

events as a barometer, gauging the growth of public sentiment keenly, and particularly watching the development of the new industries and new resources. He accentuated the American idea in everything he undertook.

There was something sublime in the way in which he viewed his defeat in the tariff reform cyclone of 1892. I often discussed the situation with him — and then we talked of the " McKinley Bill." I remember how his eyes sparkled when it was suggested that his bill was the sole cause of Republican defeat, and how he delivered a statement to me with an air of prophecy:

" That may have been so, but the bill was passed so short a time prior to election that it was easy for our opponents to make charges and there was no time for us to combat them; but wait and see, Mark — wait and see. The principles and policies of that bill will yet win a greater victory for our party than we have ever had before. This misunderstanding will yet contribute to overwhelming Republican success."

The general conditions were such, however,

that the party's reverse could not be attributed entirely to the McKinley Bill. There were other factors in the landslide of '92.

During the early part of the campaign of 1896 the charge was made that McKinley voted for the free coinage of silver. And with his usual candor he admitted that, in the earlier stages of the agitation of the money question, it was to him then a proposition he had not fully investigated; he did not pretend to be a doctor of finance and had followed the popular trend of that time. After fuller discussion and practical demonstration of facts; after observing the changing conditions of the country, and weighing the question in its various relations to the fundamental laws of practical finance and the true policy best for the country, his conclusions were voiced in the St. Louis platform of 1896.

The last discussion that I had with him upon the money question before he was nominated was a few days before I left for St. Louis, at my office in Cleveland.

He turned to my desk, sat down and wrote

in lead pencil an article which he handed me
when finished, saying:

" There, Mark, are my ideas of what our
platform should be on the money question."

I carried the paper in my pocket to St. Louis
some days before the convention, and that
declaration of William McKinley contained in
substance what was afterward drafted into
the plank in the platform on that question. I
mention this because in subsequent discussion
a great deal has been said about the construc-
tion of that plank in the St. Louis platform on
the tariff and money question.

This absolute declaration was given me by
Major McKinley as embracing his ideas, and
while the language may have been changed
somewhat, the meaning of the article he wrote
weeks before the convention was absolutely
followed in the platform of 1896.

As to the quality of his courage, I never
knew a man more fearless. In the dark days
of the Ohio gerrymander, when, as author of
the McKinley Bill, he lost his seat in congress,
he was cheerful in a defeat that had cut a
Democratic majority of 2,000 down to 300. He

had fought an uphill fight, and although de-
feated was elated over the confidence which
his home people expressed in the principles
which he represented. The defeat had no de-
pressing effect on his mind and energies, but
spurred him to greater effort. And in every
serious emergency that confronted him he
was prepared for the event — always calm
and courageous. Even amidst the onslaughts
of campaign abuse he never uttered in my
presence one retaliatory word, but always
referred to the enemy as " our opponents,"
while I must confess I used stronger adjectives
at times.

———

There was nothing that he enjoyed more
than a social time with friends at dinner. He
always entered into the spirit of the occasion
and contributed his full share of merriment.
And once aroused he showed a side of his character that few were acquainted with. He enjoyed jokes to the full measure, and was a pleasant tease. When he once had a joke on me he
rang all the changes; and no one enjoyed a
joke on himself more thoroughly than he did.

In 1897, when I was a tenderfoot, recently arrived in Washington, he asked me to give up a dinner engagement with some gentlemen to fill up the table as an emergency man at a dinner to be given at the White House that night. I declined, saying I had a better thing — not knowing that an invitation to the White House was equivalent to a command. This joke on me was a delight to him.

When he was a guest at my house for several days, or a member of a house party, his flow of genial spirits began at the breakfast table and continued uninterrupted all day. He seemed to feel as if he were on a vacation, and had the joyous spirit of a big boy home from school, always looking after the comfort of others, with never, apparently, a thought for himself. An ideal home-body was William McKinley, and the American fireside was a shrine of worship with him.

At one of our house parties we had a flash-light photograph taken of the dinner guests. He was particularly fond of this dinner picture because it contained a splendid likeness of Mrs. McKinley.

When McKinley laughed, he laughed heartily all over, and was a perfect boy in his enjoyment. In all the social visits to my home, it was an inspiration to me to see the way he could throw off the cares of the day. It always made me feel twenty years younger to spend a social evening with him, and I cannot begin to measure the depth and value of this friendship to me entirely aside from his public career.

———

He was never much inclined, I believe, to take an active part in athletics, though his simple, normal habits of life kept him always in excellent condition physically and mentally. He proved the enduring sturdiness of his frame by his hard service in the Civil War, and by the tremendous amount of labor which he afterward put into the study and presentation of public questions. He was, of course, interested in the notable athletic contests that the college boys held, but it was as late as 1894 that he and I witnessed together our first game of football — a Princeton-Yale game at New York.

It was a drizzling, cold day, but he watched every movement of the game from the club-house with as keen interest as he gave to a debate in congress.

When some mysterious movement in a "pile-up" was made he would turn and ask me about it, but I had to shake my head and confess it was my first game and that it was all Greek to me.

He told me how he felt like the country boy who went to a college football game for the first time, to see the "real thing." When asked how he liked it, the country boy naively replied :

"They didn't have no game; they got into a scrap and kept fightin' all the time when they ought to have been playing ball."

At this football game there was little to foreshadow what was written in the political horizon two years later, but I do recall that he seemed to be especially popular with the sturdy young collegians, one of whom remarked to his companion as they passed by us:

"Who is that distinguished looking man — the one that looks like Napoleon?"

The late President was particularly fond of
a good play, and when he would come to stay
with me at Cleveland over night, he would always inquire: "Is there anything good at your
opera house tonight, Mark?"

We enjoyed many pleasant evenings together. He delighted in meeting the prominent actors, and was very fond of Joseph
Jefferson. Many an hour have they chatted
together, and Jefferson never failed to call
and see him when in Washington. Sol Smith
Russell was another friend. The drama of
high standard was to him a relief from worri-
ments of the day and thoroughly enjoyed as
a relaxation. He delighted to discuss with
these play-folks their art, and how actors, like
men in public life, had to cater to public wishes
and how much their influence meant in pro-
ducing plays of healthful purpose and moral
teaching. Mrs. McKinley was also very fond
of the theater; he always delighted to indulge
her, and they spent many happy evenings together witnessing the best plays that were on
the boards.

He never tired of seeing Jefferson in "Rip

Van Winkle" and "The Cricket on the Hearth," which were undoubtedly his favorite plays.

"Mark, you meet as many distinguished men as owner of an opera house as you do as Senator," he would jokingly remark after a chat with an actor. He always seemed to have a keen scent for talent in any profession and was quick to recognize genius. The psychological study the actor made in portraying human nature before the footlights was to him fascinating. The personality of these men on the stage he believed had a potent influence on the public mind. He never tired of high-class dramas; he was especially fond of Shakespeare's plays, and always attended thoroughly "read up." He would often chide me for not being more carefully posted on the original Shakespearean text, but I was most concerned in the play as staged.

How well I remember how he enjoyed witnessing the play entitled "The Politician," during his second campaign for governor of Ohio. We sat together in a box. Roland Reed, who played the "Politician" and who is now dead, directed his remarks straight at us, and

McKinley enjoyed his hits immensely. The actor brought in impromptu points and so generously improvised the speaking part that it seemed as if the actors and audience were having an " aside " all to themselves at our expense.

———

A man of more generous impulses than William McKinley never lived. When cases were presented to him for relief that were beyond his ability to meet, he would apply to me or some of his friends for assistance in aiding worthy persons, and his friends were always glad to respond to these appeals. He was liberal without stint. It gave him actual physical pain to see anyone suffering or in distress, and on such occasions he showed his great faith in friendship, never hesitating to go to any bounds in an appeal for others. Whatever he had in his pocket, whether it was ten cents or ten dollars, he was always ready to give it to relieve distress. If the applicant only required fifty cents and the Major had ten dollars in his pocket, the applicant would get the ten. He did not know such a thing as taking change from charity.

Though he had no especial training in music, no person was more partial to it than William McKinley. And his tastes were as catholic as a child's. Anything from a hurdygurdy to grand opera pleased him. He would keep his hands or feet beating time whenever there was music about him. I recall many Sunday evening home concerts. Every one was singing, and he would call for "Nearer, my God, to Thee" and "Lead, Kindly Light." The radiance on his face when he sang those old favorite hymns, as if his whole soul was in it, is to me a sacred memory picture of William McKinley.

He would urge me to try to sing and insisted I had a sweet tenor voice, but the pleasant charm of the happy occasions was never marred by my vocal efforts.

I knew I could not sing, but I listened; the echoes of those happy hours will linger with me as long as I live. The little singing parties in our home after dinner were always his delight.

I had the closest revelations of William

McKinley's character, I think, in our quiet hours of smoking and chatting, when all the rest had retired. Far past midnight we have sat many times talking over those matters which friends always discuss — and the closer I came to the man, the more lovable his character appeared. Every time we met there was revealed the gentle, growing greatness of a man who knew men, respected them and loved them. Never was it the personal interests of William McKinley that he discussed, but those of friends, or his party, and above all, of the people. His clear-cut conscientiousness was pronounced. In these heart-to-heart talks — friend to friend — in the calm serenity of the night's quiet hours, we felt the ties of our life's friendship growing stronger as we simply sat and puffed and looked in each other's faces. These home smoke-chats are the treasured memories of a man who loved mankind much more than he did himself and who had consecrated his career to the people. He always was interested in business and industrial affairs and understood them as few men did in their relation to the home comforts and happiness of the American people. It was in these quiet hours together that the splendid devotion of the man to high and noble ideals showed clearest. I think that a reminiscent glance at our smoke-chat meetings night after night, wherever we chanced to be, reveals to me most freely the great qualities in the man whom the world has so profoundly honored. I can see that kindly, quizzical look in his deep blue eyes under his bushy eyebrows, when he broke the silence after meditating:

"Mark, this seems to be right and fair and just. I think so, don't you?" His "don't you?" or "did you?" always had a tone that invited candid confidence, and this is a peculiarity that brings back to my memory some incidents of our acquaintanceship in early years that seemed to foreshadow his future.

Looking back over the long years of association with William McKinley, nothing seems to stand out more prominently than the hearty and sunny way in which he always enjoyed the friendly hours of recreation. These pleasant episodes of a purely personal nature are emphasized more and more as I think of him, and it is these that I most cherish in the memory of the man. His greatness as a statesman was but the reflection of his greatness as a man.

William McKinley was faultless in his friendships.

III. In the White House.

I came to Washington a few days in advance of the inauguration in 1897 to make the final arrangements as chairman of the National Committee. How well I remember the morning of McKinley's arrival, as I went to the Ebbitt House to meet him. He had stopped at this hotel for many years as a Congressman, and was now a guest as President. I was particularly impressed on meeting the same McKinley that I had seen so often before in his room at the hotel while a member of Congress. There was nothing in his manner or appearance to denote that any change whatever had come over him; there was nothing in his expression of the exultation of success or political victory or personal prestige. If there was any difference it was that he appeared to me more serious, more warmly sympathetic, in the gentle dignity that came upon him under the weight of the great responsibilities before him. It would have taken a close observer to discover that he was other than the old member of Congress from Ohio quietly assuming the duties and responsibilities of an everyday routine in the work which he loved. He greeted me with the same sweet smile and hearty handshake which I had known so well for thirty years past, and I could scarcely realize that he had become the ruler of the greatest nation on earth and that he was still to remain the same confidential and loving friend as in the old days.

After the pomp and ceremony of the inauguration was over he appeared to slip into his place with an ease and grace that told the story to every one over again that had been proclaimed so effectively during the campaign just closed, — that William McKinley, of all men, at this time exactly "fitted the situation."

———

Immediately after Congress was called in extraordinary session in 1897, to begin the business in hand, to fulfill the promises made by the Republican party. The changed conditions of the country seemed to engross his concentrated attention day after day, hour after hour, morning, noon and night. In all his talk and conversation with me there was one supreme purpose, and that was to bring the nation back to the old anchorage of sound money and a protective policy. His work from day to day was laid out with the system and care of an architect or an artisan who had specific duties before him. The Dingley Bill ? was almost ready for the House, and in shaping and advising along this policy, keeping in mind prosperity for the people as the one great desired object, he was always at his best and always enthusiastic. For the first few months of his administration his whole time was taken up in dealing with a proposition concerning which he was an acknowledged expert, and more than that, involving a labor of love which seemed to be more apparent in his work than a sense of perfunctorily performing executive duties. He was, in fact, enthusiastic in this work and had a happy, cheery way of meeting old friends as well as new acquaintances that had always stood by him in so many fights for the principles of protection; happy especially because in every outstretched hand that came to greet him there was a pledge of loyalty and support which made him feel strong and fixed in his determination to do his utmost for his country's good.   It was not merely a generalized or theorized purpose of patriotism that inspired him; he appeared always to have the specific and concrete interest of the people as individuals in mind when he undertook to solve the great questions of public welfare.

In those days his social life was a happy one because his dear wife caught the inspiration of the work in hand and in the new environment her own life had been brightened.   She was personally interested in those things which have made the White House a bright reflection of ideal American home life.   Her interest in those matters was especially appreciated by the devoted husband, who seemed to feel that the great purpose of all American policies should concentrate in the betterment of conditions of the American home and fireside.

After the adjournment of Congress, about the first of August, 1897, the President took a much-needed vacation of a few weeks, but during all that time was constantly engrossed with work. He never seemed to quite throw off the serious purpose that had been interwoven in all the acts of his public career. Immediately after his return to Washington he began the preparation of outlining in written data and notes the fixed ideas expressing his own line of policy which was destined to be of so great benefit to his country and to humanity as well. When Congress reassembled in December, 1897, he had fully made his forecast and was prepared to meet in a masterful way the questions of the hour.

The country knows only too well how quickly he grasped the serious situation that came up later in the island of Cuba and led to the outbreak of the Spanish war. It was during these trying days that I saw President McKinley in a new light. As difficulties multiplied and responsibilities increased he seemed to grow even more masterful and self-reliant. As close as we had been as personal friends, each day seemed to unfold some hitherto unobserved strength of character and nobility of purpose.

Under these conditions, I was forcibly reminded of the criticisms that had been made at an earlier time when his candidacy for the presidency was discussed. It was claimed that McKinley was a man of a single idea; that he was an expert on tariff matters only and that his claims to statesmanship were confined to his advocacy of the policies and principles of protection. Later developments proved this to be far from the truth. There was not a detail or a situation in any branch of the government with which he came into contact that he did not fully fathom and master. The intricate and unprecedented questions growing out of the war situation he met in much the same way that he did as a young lawyer in solving the intricacies of the case before him. While he had a loyal and efficient cabinet, he always led in the newer propositions presented. His judgment never faltered, nor did he fail to awaken enthusiastic support in all with whom he came into contact. In fact, his influence with men grew so strong that the whole Congress of the United States was ready to follow his leadership in all matters pertaining to the conduct of the war, having perfect faith in his patriotism, tried and true, and his ability, which had time and again withstood the crucial test.

One of the remarkable things concerning his whole administration was this personal confidence and esteem which he universally inspired and so well earned from every man of both political parties in the Congress of the United States. In all the upheavals brought about by the conditions and new questions growing out of the war, the problem of insular possessions and our relations with Cuba, the influence of his personality never changed or relaxed while his life lasted, and in the closing days of his public career was reached the climax of a pure and noble life.

During the hot, sultry days of August in 1898, William McKinley continued unceasingly his long hours of labor at the White House. Night after night found him at work if there were pressing matters at hand, and usually there were problems of the gravest importance demanding his attention as commander-in-chief. Often I would go over to the White House and sit with him on the south porch when he had finished his work, with various members of Congress or cabinet members, and in the long Summer evenings we would enjoy those little friendly gatherings far past midnight. He seemed to consider these brief hours of recreation as well worth the arduous labors of the long day. During these meetings he had little to say of the serious and sad things of life, but was always an optimist and his enthusiasm was infectious. He was particularly fond of telling and listening to stories and cracking jokes, always in that good-humored and gentle way which never possessed the rapier touch of satire or temper.

———

Perhaps the greatest strain upon William McKinley during his whole life was the few months prior to the declaration of war. The suspense of the situation in getting at all the facts wore upon him, and his patience under distressing circumstances always appeared to

me saintly. But when war was finally de-
clared, and the inevitable came upon us, his
whole manner changed. Everything else was
cast aside to do with all his might what had to
be done in pushing the war. He settled down
in that quiet, serious and determined way
which emphasized his mastery of the problems before him. How often I have watched
him in those thoughtful moods. He would
remain silent for some time and seeming to
commune with himself — "think it out," as
he would jokingly remark. And when he had
settled the matter fully in his own mind, his
old natural manner would come back with a
rebound and he was again the same smiling,
sweet and gentle companion.

His unvarying habit was, when advising
with any one in matters of state or serious
import, to first find out what the other fellow
thought. On this situation he always seemed
to build his premises, and he had a faculty of
getting it out of you somehow or other; sometimes he would approve and sometimes he
would say nothing, but he was always an earnest
seeker after the truth and the facts, seeming

entirely to obliterate his personal prejudices in his eagerness to arrive at a just and equitable conclusion.

———

I have often observed how he never withheld his sympathy in any case, no matter how small or inconsequential it might be. There was a particularly interesting incident in his desiring to appoint an old school friend to a small postoffice in one of the western states. The lady was a widow and needed the income toward the support of herself and family, but the Congressman had previously recommended for the position a man who had been of some service to him in his congressional campaign. For a time there was an indication of feeling growing out of the matter and it appeared like a curious commentary upon the power of the President of the United States, when he was unable to control the appointment to a fourth-class postoffice, under the inexorable unwritten law of precedent. But the situation was soon solved when the Congressman held a conference with William McKinley. The President had made an effective plea with the irritated and annoyed member, who had resented interference with his absolute prerogative when fanned into temper by outsiders; but the President won his point for the old school friend and none were more cheerful parties to the plan than the Congressman and disappointed candidate for the postoffice. They had felt the touch of human sympathy such as William McKinley could always inspire.

———

William McKinley was the incarnation of the best and purest statesmanship, which, I believe, exists in every American. His qualities that inspired in me a close personal friendship were given with the same unstinted grace and generosity to every individual that came within the influence of his personality, no matter how remote or how humble that individual might be. His career is a treasured heritage of the human race, and marks the beginning of a new epoch in the history of the United States.

mr Kulg assassination